Here Is Why I Failed

ASIF BASHEER

HERE IS WHY I FAILED

Copyright © 2012 Asif Basheer

All rights reserved.

ISBN: 9798356359095

DEDICATION

I dedicate this short book, to all the failures that taught me lessons that my MBA did not.

HERE IS WHY I FAILED

CONTENTS

	Acknowledgments	i
1	Here is Why I Failed	6
2	How It Began	Pg 8
3	Mistake 1: The Art of Delegation	Pg 10
4	Mistake 2: Perspective	Pg 18
5	Mistake 3: Product	Pg 24
6	Mistake 4: Plan	Pg 30
7	Mistake 5: Time tested structures	Pg 36
8	Bonus: Mistake 6 - Procrastination	Pg 40
9	Conclusion	Pg 44
10	Links To Follow	Pg 48
11	About the Author	

HERE IS WHY I FAILED

ACKNOWLEDGMENTS

Thank God, for making me commit all those mistakes. Huge thank you to my parents for letting me be who I am. Thanks a ton, Krishna, for putting up with my fuss over the nitty gritties and delays in response, while editing this. Thank you Nishanth and Renjith, for helping with the cover design. Huge shoutout to all my clients(former and current) for everything.

1 Here Is Why I Failed

I failed.

I failed.

I failed.

I failed not once, but thrice.

In my 4 years long entrepreneurial journey, I had the good fortune to fail three times and adding to it was the fact that I'm an engineering dropout.

Why did I use the word "good fortune"? Because this book does not depict how big the failures were nor does it lament their impacts. But portrays how our attitude towards it made a difference. This book is to show why I failed as a bootstrapped business founder while venturing into a start-up right after an epiphany that stemmed from my experience at the job I had back then.

HERE IS WHY I FAILED

When I got a job right out of college, I thought it was a huge achievement because back then all I had was a bachelor's degree (a course I joined after dropping from engineering). I wasn't exactly a newcomer when it came to business.-I had started out young, trying to hone my skills. So when I joined the new job I had a little experience from running an event management business and selling academic books from my college days. But soon I wanted to go on my own and shifted my focus.

Starting up is the easiest part. With technology at our fingertips and the abundant opportunities out there, anybody can easily set up a business these days. All you need is a product that the market needs and a plan to get through to the customer's pulse.

I started with my first venture the same way. I dived into the market with a service but it was a product that n number of others were already offering in market. Unfazed by the competition, I stood confident, as I believed that I could get clients right from the start. This confidence (now thinking back, over-confidence) was cemented by a couple of incidents of early success. But the very same early success soon led to an early burn.

2 How It Began

Fresh out of my first job, I started Asta Ventures. Today it stands tall as an IT recruitment and performance management business for startups and SMBs. About 2 years into running Asta Ventures, I relaunched my previous college startup, this time as Webvendere Solutions, a full-stack digital agency offering digital marketing, web and mobile development and design services. Today we offer our services to clients across the globe, irrespective of big or small the company is.

How did I reach here?

It wasn't a path filled with roses. Over the years, I have come to know that with failures come realizations. I started to introspect. I learned my lessons the hard way but I have taken care since to not repeat them.

Here, I am sharing five of my biggest mistakes that I initially overlooked. These lead to my failures, but they also taught me the biggest lessons that paved the way to better myself and perfect my craft.

HERE IS WHY I FAILED

3 MISTAKE 1: THE ART OF DELEGATION

HERE IS WHY I FAILED

'Hey, I need a favour.'

'Yes, what?'

'I want you to take care of my business for a short while. Not much, but around… maybe 30 days. Will be back in the office next month. I need to be away for something important. Will you please take care of the operations while I'm away?'

'I'm not sure how I would fit into your shoes!'

'You know how to run a business, right? I called you since you are on a sabbatical after your last startup.'

'Yeah, I'm very well aware of how the business works.'

'See, I knew it. That's why I called you.'

'But I'm not sure how I can handle it as you do. You would be better off if you would look for someone to handle the operations.'

'See, I'm running against the clock to make sure the things over here would run smoothly and I'm out of bandwidth to hire people within a week. Even if I manage to hire someone, I will still have to train and manage them. With my current situation, it's better if there's someone like you to handle the operations. Try to help out. Please!'

'Ok. I will try my best, but I am not sure though.'

'Please, it would be great if you can come aboard and handle stuff for a short while and keep the clients posted. I will pay you 40k for the month.'

'Let me see.'

HERE IS WHY I FAILED

People are the most valuable assets in any business. Be it a hotel or a hospital, sports school or a superstore, people make the business work. I ventured into my first proper business as a solopreneur operation with just my time and network as the capital.

A few years before that, my first business, while I was still in college, was a textbook sales gig that I started with my buddy, Abraham. While we took it from our classroom to across the college and beyond, Abraham had my back. On the other hand, in my solopreneur debut, Asta Ventures, the operations were slated for transforming it into a full-blown HR agency, once there was a regular stream of revenue from the initial crop of stable clients. We got our first client on day one of being in business. They were clients of my previous employer, but when I started out, they believed in me enough to come on board with me. For the next six months, we toiled day and night, handling rejections daily, and going all in on the business.

But that six months of sweat and tears took the company from a single person working with startups, to SMBs and corporates across the nation. In its first eight months of operations, the business grew from my bedroom to 3 cities, all the while closing impactful positions across multiple levels of expertise. My months were split between the cities we were operational in.

However, even as the business grew, I made a mistake- the mistake of thinking that I could keep the show going all by myself.

I shied from hiring more people, for the fear of a productivity drop. I was reluctant to hire more people, less than a year into the business, even when the workload was taking a toll on me. I could easily have afforded to hire 2 team members, without hurting the business finances.

HERE IS WHY I FAILED

That's where it all came crashing down.

A personal engagement, a road accident, and the rest period that followed forced me to stay away from the business for two months. The business plummeted from having clients across the country to having zero clients and resources. I went back to square one. When I started the business, I had the safety net of the savings from my job at Gencom, but now, I was broke after burning through the savings in 8 months and no runway. Broke with no revenue or clients.

Why?

Because I had no one to delegate work to.

While I was away, business took a hit. I went from high-performance mode to square one, without a runway. I regret that I could have saved the business if I had a small team which could have managed the day-to-day operations and kept the business going while I was away. A last-minute search for someone might have cushioned the downfall, had there been someone to take up the slack and hold it till I was back.

The first thing that I did in my second innings was to find a co-founder, an HR professional with almost 10 years of experience who had previously worked with both nationally and internationally renowned companies. A co-founder gave me the assurance that even when I was away, the business had someone at the helm to manage it.

We hired a solid team of recruiters who have since stood by our side.

With the latest additions to the team, we have our products and services developed in line with the needs of various target users. And with the right people aboard, we plan to handle the hire-to-fire cycle and change how job seekers become employed.

We have only one motto now: at Asta Ventures and Webvendere, your status as a graduate doesn't matter; whether you possess the right skills matter because at the end of the day, I need people I can trust in a crisis.

HERE IS WHY I FAILED

4 MISTAKE 2: PERSPECTIVE

HERE IS WHY I FAILED

Initially, I was super confident about what I could and couldn't do. Once the business became operational, I started learning everything I could lay my hands on. The learning curve was steep, but I enjoyed it. From a mundane desk job, my days took a 360-degree turn where I started to learn, unlearn and relearn everything required to float the boat and keep the revenue going. Learning new skills and experimenting with them helped a lot in the initial phase.

But three months into the process, my mindset started to change from a learner's perspective to an execution perspective, where I started diving into projects with little to no research or learning.

That change in attitude brought a huge change in my approach to everything, albeit a negative one. My growth mindset took a back seat with a know-it-all attitude taking the steering, and with that came the boss mindset. It set the scene for multiple business disasters and huge revenue losses; eye-openers that forced me to stop and look at myself. How I incurred such huge losses was a puzzle for me back then, but now, I know where I faltered, and where I committed mistakes I should never have - I had fallen into a mindset an entrepreneur could easily develop but should never have, and that ranked first on my list of mistakes.

The change of mindset from 'growing with knowledge' to 'know-it-all' happened so fast that I had thought of myself as an overnight success when in reality,

I was an absolute nobody.

Fortunately, the insight that everything was spiraling down came at the right time. I could take corrective actions before everything went out of hand. One meeting with a prospect made me realize that I was neck-deep in trouble and had been oblivious to the fact.

He showed me a mirror about how exactly my business was going.

I did not like what I saw.

It got me thinking.

That meeting made me introspect and do a mindset shift.

Redemption started when I got a chance to take a look at a dear friend's accounts, who was freelancing at the time. He was doing better without all the bells and whistles I had. The realization that he was getting things right with almost less than half the resources I had, puzzled me.

Pondering over the biggest question- why - soon switched the light bulb on.

And that sparked the change.

Going back to the learner/growth mindset was the best thing that happened to me after all the setbacks. It gave better clarity of what was going wrong with my business and how I was the root cause of all the hurdles in my path. Around that time (like any other entrepreneur), I got hold of a copy of *The One Thing* by Peter Thiel. That book taught me that I need to quit running after 10 shiny things at the same time and start focusing on one thing that mattered the most. This switch brought the most impactful change in my businesses and in me as a person.

I became more focused and sought out knowledge actively, which helped improve business processes and life in general. From being in a state of zero productivity and binge-watching movies after my first failure, I shifted my focus to the next task to do.

I started investing time to improve myself. And the change was not limited to me but to my entire team. The entire team was upskilled with training from an industry professional from the client industry, so we had better clarity on what we are working on. The practice of team orientation continues now, irrespective of whether they are freelancers or full-time team members.

I have ingrained the one-task motto to the point where now my day starts with figuring out the one most important task for the day so that I can get that done, no matter what. Once that **One Task of the Day** is done, the urge to perform and bring the best experience for the clients and candidates motivates everyone in my team, and, most importantly me, to work on areas that need improvement. It pushes us to learn new skills to better ourselves professionally and to be a better version of ourselves.

When we set out to plan our next project, this became our primary rule. We want to bring forward a set of job seekers who are built different, who are smart, and not just another resume to the job market. And for that, the rule we have set in stone is to get them to focus on one thing that matters to them to secure their job. Most job seekers fresh out of college tend to follow the herd and become a nobody in the job market.

With the latest advancements in AI and HR tech, the attention spans of recruiters have become shorter than ever and have come to the point where the resume that stands out in front of a recruiter gets a call unless the candidate possesses niche skills in demand and we make sure our candidates stand out and stands tall among his competitors.

HERE IS WHY I FAILED

5 MISTAKE 3: PRODUCT

HERE IS WHY I FAILED

"Hello, this is Arun, from Marinex Shipping, Kochi (company name changed for client confidentiality). Is this Asta Ventures?"

"Yes, How may I help you?"

"We are into shipping and freight forwarding services. Our client base is mostly based out in North America and the Middle East. At times we work with clients and employ 2-3 offshore teams for our clients, to handle their food supply logistics once they hit the Indian waters and dock at the major ports. We are now looking forward to hiring an HR Manager with experience handling international client accounts and with excellent communication skills to interact with them. The requirement is for a Dubai-based client of ours. We prefer someone with shipping industry experience. If that's hard to find, people with experience in logistics companies in the maritime sector are also fine. Can you help us out?"

"Sure, sir."

"How do you charge for your services?"

"Our usual rate is 8.33% of annual CTC."

"Cool."

"It would be great if you can share the requirement details. Will text you our email address now. Please share the details there and we can get things started soon."

"Sure thing. Thank you."

Call disconnects.

I sat there wondering what was I even doing. Shipping was an alien industry till then.

For every prospect out there, regardless of their industry, my agency was a recruitment firm that introduced them to the right job seekers across all levels of expertise and experience. We were excited about the work. Once the initial adrenaline subsided, I realized that this policy was taking us nowhere. It took me some time to make myself understand that it was unsustainable to be offering every other service under the sun.

Serving clients across sectors like IT, ITeS, FMCG, Realty, BPO/KPO, Sales, Food and Beverages, Manufacturing and more, placing candidates from freshers to seniors, gave the adrenaline rush while being on the jetpack.

Little did I know that my jetpack was on fire and leaking fuel, at 1000ft above a canyon, with a parachute full of gaping holes.

Being everywhere doesn't help any business to grow exponentially, be it in any industry. One particular incident with a BPO client, one of the largest in the country, had us being embarrassed by them for promising the service delivery and under- delivering. After the first failure, we changed just one thing. But that changed everything for the agency.

We narrowed ourselves down to just one niche. From n number of niches, we started focusing on just one sector. While the breakup with other industries was painful, we had to let them go.

The focus shifted from everything to just the IT sector.

That one simple change made everything beautiful.

From juggling between services while being unable to give our 100%, to having specific things to do, made sure the team stayed productive.

We learned to say no.

Niching down cemented the saying that riches are in the niches, for us. What used to be getting 15-20 low ticket closures every month became 5-10 high ticket closures that made the revenue grow by 8-10x.

One simple change in the sectors we handled brought down the workload for us by 60% and boosted the results by 50%. One niche at a time, we are becoming better by the day now. Currently, Asta Ventures helps startups and corporates alike to recruit the best of talent, without having to go the traditional route.

Off to new markets now.

HERE IS WHY I FAILED

6 MISTAKE 4: PLAN

HERE IS WHY I FAILED

Another mistake I made was not having a proper plan on how to run the business and figuring out how to take the business forward. Every day, I was doing impromptu tasks that came along and getting random results for the business. Good results came in just when I needed them. Looking back, I cannot help but think that the business just chanced upon being there at the right places at the right times. Good things got served on just the right occasions because great results happened for visibly no reason.

Having no plan made sure that the small successes clouded any chances of devising a long-term plan to take the business forward. The casual approach that growth will happen just like every other result, paved the way for serious setbacks. There was no plan in place to keep the business on track and, more importantly, to keep me grounded. The journey till then was hopping from one fragile opportunity to another. Without a plan, the business was everywhere, and I was doing everything I could to make sure things stayed afloat.

Had there been a proper plan for what to do at each stage of the business, the business wouldn't have failed the way it did. So when I started out again we had a solid plan to get back on our feet. Going back to the drawing board meant just one thing for us. Better clarity on what we were doing wrong till then and to decide on the next step to take the business forward. With the learnings from the first failure, we as a team decided to cross one hurdle at a time, with careful, planned strides.

A 2-year plan was prepared to start a new vertical and scale the existing verticals. We now had a clear plan to get the business to scale and start new operations bases in Bengaluru and Dubai.

Just when things were working out as planned, when all the pieces of the puzzle were falling into the right places, one thing that we never planned for happened: in Wuhan, China.

COVID-19 broke out and almost all our clients went from hiring to layoffs. Just like that, we were out of business due to something that was beyond our control. There was nothing we could do but stare at the bleak business environment during the pandemic. Since the second outage did not happen from our end, we decided to wait it out, till the situation cleared. The business went to almost zero revenue for consecutive months. Even when things were uncertain, the decision to wait it out was backed by the entire team going as far as to take voluntary pay cuts.

That turned out to be the best decision we took.

When the pandemic-related restrictions started to lift, the clients started hiring again, this time at much higher numbers to satisfy their increased client requirements. The pandemic validated the relevance of digital business channels and that translated to more positions for us to close.

Until then, we did not have a contingency plan in place, but COVID-19 changed it all.

Even though the pandemic did not change how we worked (we had been a remote- work business from day one), it gave us a different perspective on how we could work differently.

After drafting a long-term plan and breaking it down into multiple short-term plans, one of our interns asked a question - what would we do if one of the points in the long-term plan did not work out due to certain market conditions (like a recession or change in technology adoption, etc.) It was a question that we were not prepared to answer. That made us create a contingency plan for all the long and short-term plans.

With the plans came SOPs to put these plans into action. The SOPs made sure everyone on the team had a clearly assigned set of job roles, unlike before, when everyone used to do everything. As I write this, the team is developing an updated version of the SOP to include the provision to transition willing freelancers to an almost full-time engagement with the business. This change helps us have a hybrid model of employment for freelancers, for them to have a regular stream of work while keeping the freedom they have in freelancing. A simple way of ensuring that our people grow with us.

HERE IS WHY I FAILED

7 MISTAKE 5: TIME-TESTED STRUCTURES

Since the business started out as a solopreneur operation, things were planned and executed as things came along. Tasks were all in my head and not even written anywhere.

With every step of growth, I devoted more and more hours to my work. It reached a stage where apart from when I was asleep, I was working. But in the tide of adrenaline, I overlooked the simple fact that it was draining my health physically and mentally.

Being the only person involved and responsible, work started piling up pretty fast and, many a time was left unfinished. The productivity dropped and work became boring. What used to be exciting and enjoyable in the beginning had by then become boring and tiresome. The drive, the insane urge to grow, was lost somewhere.

This led to more work being unfinished and gave me a serious bout of productivity guilt. For almost 3 months, the amount of work completed was close to zero.

The focus was gone for good, and every time I sat down to work, I ended up watching another episode and eventually, all the seasons of The Office. For almost 90 days, I stayed glued to my screen watching the likes of Silicon Valley, Dark, Hostel Daze, etc. I neared completion with my Netflix watch list and a long list of movies and sitcoms I had previously skipped.

We did not have a proper structure of proven system and this, unfortunately, ensured one thing- getting the business back on its feet was an uphill task if the state of affairs remained the way it was.

The first thing we did on the second outing was to plan and implement a structured system that could keep the business running and could take it forward.

HERE IS WHY I FAILED

On the personal side, building a second brain was one thing that made a world of change- where all the tasks and methods were logged with tools and systems that made sure I never forgot anything.

From day 1 of the second outing, every enquiry that came in went through a vetting process that made sure the lead was good to chase. All the leads that cleared the screening were followed up with implementing a proper CRM (Thanks to an Agile CRM for making it possible).

For a full list of SaaS tools we use at our businesses, follow the links on the Business tools page.

Meetings were scheduled only for those prospects who were really interested in working with us and could afford our fees. The pace of client onboarding slowed down after the screening implementation, but the ticket sizes climbed up. On the operations side of things, a structured system was put into action after brainstorming with our recruiter team. Even though it was slightly heavier on the pocket than before, the system eased everyone's workload and increased the task completion rate.

As mentioned earlier, if we used to fill in 15-20 client requirements in a month before, now it came down to 8-10 positions, but the revenue per closure started climbing. With the systems in place, the team had something to follow and keep track of. Each team now had a designated role. Post closure, all the client-side communication till billing got assigned to the business development team, with a simple hack- they started getting incentives for it. The follow-up and billing duty was initially split between the co-founders and the accounts team but with this approach, we relieved our accounts team of following-up raised invoices and payments to be received and the business development team happily took it over.

In 3 months, we had the team working at maximum productivity, with an hour per day devoted to learning and improving their skill sets.

Another major change that helped the team become productive was transferring a good number of entry-level positions to our newly created freelancer panel. Our freelancer team made sure we had a regular flow of candidates for entry-level positions and minimal snags. We now have a strong panel of freelancers who support us and grow with us.

Follow the link at the end to join our freelancer panel, if you are a freelance recruiter.

With a strong team of freelancers and full-time team members, we are now creating a system that works like a well-oiled machine that seldom stops or stutters and gives the best output. Another best decision that worked for us was taking the advice of Tim Ferris. After reading *4-Hour Workweek* by Tim Ferris (one of the many ways Tim Ferris influenced me), the workweek went from 6 to 5 days. This was another book that had a positive impact on how we build systems that gave optimal output with productive effort.

One experience of all the issues that stemmed from the lack of proper systems at Asta Ventures ensured I had a system to implement and execute while starting up my second business, Webvendere Solutions.

Off we go, putting the plans into action!

8 MISTAKE 6: PROCRASTINATION (BONUS)

HERE IS WHY I FAILED

Apart from the mistakes mentioned already, there were multiple other mistakes that added to the misery.

Procrastination was the root cause of most of the issues.

Being a master procrastinator, I was always keeping things to the last minute and was always overloaded with work. Just like how compounding works in wealth, compounding worked in my case too, in quickly escalating the issues from small ones, to one dangerous issue.

Lack of proper and timely communication was one of the by-products of procrastination that ensured the failure. One instance where a client, who we will name Ganesh (from one of the largest business software companies in India), insulted us, albeit jokingly, in front of a group of prospects at a networking event, saying it takes at least a century for us to call or send a mail to inform them of any update(which was partially true). They did not terminate the contract since the work was getting done even if delayed, and the delivered work was of the best possible quality. But it was an instance of forceful eye-opening to me.

Since I was the point of contact between the updates coming from my recruiter and the client, the communication broke almost always at my end. Even while working towards growth and scaling up, client communications suffered because of my procrastination. Keeping it all in my head was the practice and once it all got too much, forgetting tasks became a daily affair.

For every important task, be it sending a message/email or calling someone to give an update on the work progress, it took a long time for the task to be done. While I would be so sure of the importance and urgency of it, it always ended up being forgotten (after making mental notes to complete the task and keeping it for later).

Getting over my procrastination was the primary step I took to change after the first and second failures. It was not an easy task and I have been putting every effort to change things for the better, for a long time. I can now say that I am slowly but steadily overcoming my procrastination after getting an accountability partner who keeps track of my to-do list and makes sure the work gets done on time, every time.

9 CONCLUSION

HERE IS WHY I FAILED

Through the ups and downs, we are constantly learning things and experimenting on the go, to become better versions of ourselves. At the time of writing this book, both my businesses, Asta Ventures, and Webvendere Solutions are doing better than I had planned while starting out. Every setback was a learning experience that gave a lesson to learn.

My single-person businesses are now backed by a core team of 13, who believed in me even at my lowest and stood by my side. Now we grow together.

At Asta Ventures, the operations at Bengaluru that was shut at the onset of COVID-19 is to be relaunched soon, with a new team and a new process. We are launching 3 different platforms soon that will cater to jobseekers and employers. Webvendere Solutions is now scaling the services business up and getting into SaaS products for freelancers and SMBs. As we had once dreamt, our business is flying high with strategic tie-ups with clients across the Middle East, UK, Europe and Australia.

Getting the right people and not just the best people aboard is one thing we focus on now, since people are the best assets any business can have. A majority of our team members might not have a college degree but they are among the best in their trade. I myself am a mechanical engineering dropout but the key is I eventually managed to figure out what I could and couldn't do.

Having a co-founder was the next best thing I did after starting up. It freed me from a lot of tasks that I had limited knowledge of and had to learn on the go to manage the projects at hand. At Asta Ventures, getting my co-founder aboard made sure the day- to-day operations are taken care of even when I'm away. Getting my technical co-founder at Webvendere did wonders with how we completed projects. Before that, I used to be managing digital marketing operations (my strong forte) as well as managing development projects (my weak point). Now, even when I'm away from the office for client-side assignments, he ensures timely project delivery while I focus on non-technical work.

Every day is a new opportunity and we grab those as a team. We believe that a team that stays together, grows together.Here's to the vision of having a high-performance team that grows together and gets ahead in life, and the plan to take it forward.

Here's to more successful businesses and to getting started on new paths!

LINKS TO FOLLOW

- Check out the SaaS tools we use at Asta Ventures and Webvendere Solutions.

https://bit.ly/myfavesaas

- Are you a freelance recruiter? Join our freelancer panel today.

https://bit.ly/freelancerpanel

ABOUT THE AUTHOR

Asif Basheer

Asif Basheer is a Kochi based recruiter, digital marketer and entrepreneur running two businesses, Webvendere Solutions a full stack digital agency and Asta Ventures, an IT recruitment firm. A certified lazy blogger and part time podcaster, Asif talks about small business, digital marketing and SaaS tools online.

www.ingramcontent.com/pod-product-compliance
Lightning Source LLC
Chambersburg PA
CBHW030514220526
45464CB00006B/2789